In memory of my father, Walter Henry Ford
1909–1974

Appledore Rope Mats

A history and exploration of mat-making
techniques ... and memories of an
Appledore 'maid'

by

Ann and George Wells

First Published May 2009
©FW Publications, 2009

ISBN 978-0-9562279-0-4

Published by FW Publications
4 Fairway, Churchill Way, Appledore
Devon EX39 1PB

email: annwells875@btinternet.com

Produced for FW Publications by
Styus International
email: mike@stylusinternational.com

Printed by
Toptown Printers Ltd, Vicarage Lawn, Barnstaple, Devon EX32 7BN

CONTENTS

FOREWORD

In September 2008 the Funchal 500 Tall Ships Regatta was held in Falmouth, Cornwall. Whilst my husband and I were visiting Falmouth for the regatta, we decided to pay a visit to the National Maritime Museum there. After a most interesting tour of the museum we headed for the Bartlett Library which is contained within the museum. Here we hoped to ascertain if there was any information regarding the making of Appledore rope mats. Or indeed if there were any records of rope mats that had been made by people living in other seafaring communities in other parts of the country. On the day we made our visit we were fortunate that Tony Pawlyn was there. Mr. Pawlyn is head of the library and a trustee. We explained our mission, and that we were making rope mats. Mr Pawlyn and his staff were very interested in our quest and were most helpful. They searched out books on how to make intricate knots, but there were no written records regarding the making of rope mats. Mr. Pawlyn advised us that as we appeared to know more about this subject than anyone else, to go home and write a book about the subject.

Although I was never formally taught how to make an Appledore rope mat, as a child and young person growing up at home, I would watch my father very closely when he was making a 'met', as the old Appledorians use to pronounce it. And it certainly did not occur to me at that time that in later life I would be drawn to try my hand at the craft. Appledore girls were not taught to make Appledore mats. The daughters of the family were known as 'maids', and were taught how to knit Appledore jerseys or frocks as the Appledorians called them.

The maids were also taught to cook the traditional meals such as 'schooner on the rocks', which is a dish of potatoes and meat with suitable seasoning cooked in the oven for an indefinite length of time, topped up with water from time to time – this liquid would be the gravy when the meal was served. This dish was the roast dinner and was always cooked onboard ship. The cheapest cuts of meat were used such as breast of lamb, brisket or belly pork. The local delicacy of laver (*Porphyra umbilicalis*), which is a type of seaweed, and slices of belly pork, known locally as henderland bacon, was fried, served with heel taps (the local name for sliced boiled potatoes which had been fried in the bacon fat), was also a favourite meal and is still so today, especially if it is topped with a fried egg. And knubbies – mother would knock up a dozen of these every other day – is the local name given to individual sponge cakes which contain sultanas or currants.

Cooking has never been one of my favourite pastimes, though. And I did try knitting an Appledore frock once, but mother had to finish it! I have very strong hands and fingers, so she spent as much time as I did doing a few rows in order to slacken off the tightness! It was the sons, the 'boys' as they were known, of the family who were taught to make rope mats, mend and prepare nets, pull and scull boats. Some were even taught to do simple sewing repairs like darning socks or sewing on buttons. Sailors at sea always had their ditty box to hand, which contained items such as a razor for shaving, needles and thread and any other personal items which he treasured. Boys were also taught to scrape and paint the family boat, and as the Appledorian expression goes, to run the beach and pick crabs: these crabs were used as bait on fishing trips out into the estuary. It was these activities I enjoyed the most, and probably because of this, and because I had no brothers, I was treated as the boy of the family as well as being the 'maid'.

Ann Wells (née Ford)   May 2009

CHAPTER 1

The history of rope mat making

Traditionally, rope mats were made out of the old discarded ropes from the running rigging of sailing vessels or rope taken from fishing nets. Before the advent of synthetic rope, natural fibres were used, these were mainly sisal (*Agave sisalana*), manila (*Musa textilis*) or hemp (*Cannabis sativa*), also coir (*Cocos nucifera*) and cotton (genus *Gossypium*) This old rope was ideal for the mat maker to work with, as it had been barked – a process similar to the tanning of hides – which softens the rope when it is new. And it had been stretched through wear.

To alleviate prolonged periods of boredom at sea, or even time when they were unable to sail from a port because of adverse weather conditions, sailors, men on lightships and crews aboard lighthouses would fill in time between watches, or periods of prolonged calm, when the vessel did not have to be worked, with hobbies. These hobbies involved the use of materials that were to hand; old rope, pieces of wood, bones or tusks from sea mammals or fish and of course empty bottles. From these most unlikely materials, and using the most basic tools, objects of beauty were made, which today are prized by collectors all over the world; scrimshaw, ships in bottles and rope mats. Voyages on sailing ships in the 18th and 19th centuries often lasted for up to two years and perhaps even longer. Ports of call could also be months apart, especially if sailing in the Southern Ocean. It was during these long voyages that seamen and indeed sea captains began the art of rope mat making.

When a captain or seaman became dissatisfied with the prolonged separation from his family, he might come ashore and sign on a coastal sailing vessel as captain, mate or leading hand. Records show that over the years leading up to the Second World War there were still over 140 vessels registered at the ports of Barnstaple and Bideford, towns situated on the banks of the rivers Taw and Torridge, some of which had been fitted with auxiliary engines. But the main power for these old ships – as with the ocean going ships – was wind power, so the sails and the running rigging was always kept to a high standard. Nothing was ever thrown away, old rope was stored and was occasionally turned into rope fenders, some was perhaps used as frappings and, of course, some suitably sized lengths of rope would be kept to make a mat. Old canvas would have been dried and stored for other uses, some would have been cut into lengths of about six foot by about two foot wide and would have been used as a backing for a mat.

Whether the mat maker was in home waters, or 'sailing deep sea' as it was known in Appledore, there was always a time when he could get out the mat and do a few rounds. When a mat was completed, it was either taken home as a present, or was sold for baccy or beer money once in port. If the mat was taken home, because it was new it would be displayed in the front porch. Most of the houses in Appledore who had a seafarer in the family would proudly display a mat in the front porch. A goodly number of houses in Appledore have a long passageway through the house, the floor of which would be covered with mats of varying types, i.e. round, oblong or square, but they were usually all of the same size so that they would fit the width of the passageway. As the mats became worn they were relegated further and further into the house until the oldest and most tatty one would be consigned to the outhouse, so that the feet would not get chilled on the stone floor!

Contained in the archives housed at the North Devon Maritime Museum at Appledore, is the V.C. Boyle collection. This extensive collection was gathered from all over the world, and Boyle's interests were diverse and comprehensive. Amongst this collection is material regarding Appledore mats. It is a very small but most interesting part of the collection, containing as it does some beautiful drawings of Appledore mats done by Mr. Boyle. And it includes some descriptions as told to him by the men who made them. A mat was made for Mr. Boyle by Captain Tom Scilly in 1947 when the captain was aged 81. The mat took approximately 150 hours to make and the cost to Mr. Boyle was £2.10s.0d (pre-decimal), which when broken down into monetary value was 4d an hour! If today's minimum wage value of say £6 an hour was to be charged for the same amount of working hours the cost would be £900! The record shows that this mat was made of sisal, as hemp or manila were not available.

With all these ex-sea captains, sailors and fishermen living in the village making rope mats, a great deal of friendly rivalry emerged as to who could make the most intricate mat. Indeed, I have a sample of my father's work, which is very similar to the one described as made by the captain. Mr. Boyle had been told by Tom Scilly who made it for him that it was made with the use of a bicycle wheel, but I do not ever remember my father using a bicycle wheel when he made his. And, if originally the design of this mat was conjured up whilst the maker was on a long sea voyage, from where would he have got a bicycle wheel? These skills and the intricate designs were closely guarded and were passed from father to son, and by so doing it kept the know-how in the family.

Appledore: a tale of two villages

Appledore is in fact two villages which over the years have grown together, but in times gone by the two were very much separate entities. Appledore itself was on the inner side of the estuary and was, and still is, known as Point. The residents who lived here were, just slightly, a little less fierce than the residents of Irsha (now West Appledore) which is on the seaward side of the estuary. The main street through this part of the village is known as Irsha Street even today. The residents of Irsha were known as West-be-Stranders, and were considered a fierce, rough lot! But, their skills in seamanship, fishing and general knowledge of the estuary and the area around this part of the coast was unsurpassed. When a seaman had worked his way up through the ranks and had become a Master Mariner – a ship's captain – he would move from the hamlet of Irsha to one of the more substantial properties over Point: although I must add that my paternal grandfather did not, the reason being, he lived next door to the Rising Sun pub in Irsha Street! My maternal grandfather, who was also a Master Mariner, did move from Irsha street to One End Street and, after living in a house and having five children, moved up the street to number 18, or Pillar House as it was known, and then went on to have five more children. It is interesting to note here that my mother's mother went to sea with her husband in the early years of their marriage: this practice was quite normal until the children came along. There are records of whole families being lost at sea when disasters struck the old sailing vessels.

Whether he came from Irsha or Point, the skills of Appledore sailors were known in almost every port around the world, indeed when an Appledore seaman was given his discharge papers from the last ship he was on, the captain would often write at the bottom of the document that he was an Appledore man by trade. This told other sea captains that he was a competent and capable sailor who could do almost any task which was needed to be performed on board ship. Thus he was deemed to be an able seaman.

Many families had their own vessel, and the sons went to sea with their father thus learning from him his knowledge and skills. I am sure that other maritime communities functioned in just the same way.

CHAPTER 2

Materials and tools

Today it is almost impossible to acquire old used rope. When rope has been used it becomes soft and pliable making it easier to work. New rope which was being prepared for rigging or fishing nets would have been barked. This is a process akin to the tanning of hides; softening and waterproofing the rope and sail canvas and giving them that wonderful tanned look. After a few years this colouring would fade a little, but it still retained much of the softness thereby making it easy to work.

The rope which is used today for mat making are mostly natural fibres, mainly manila or hemp – some synthetic ropes are used for the more fancy pieces of work which are sometimes used for a middle of a mat. This is easier to make into what is known as a plait, because the fibres are softer and much more pliable to be made into shapes without twisting or kinking. New rope is bought in coils of two hundred and forty yards. This sounds like an awful lot of rope, but when one considers that it takes perhaps almost twenty feet of rope to make a Ocean plait for a centre design for a large oval mat, two hundred and forty yards does not appear to be to large amount.

If time is of the essence or if you are house proud, do not even consider embarking on making a rope mat. The fibres that come off the rope are spread about everywhere, and when the vacuum cleaner picks them up the contents of the bag is like an old birds nest!

■ 'Unlaying' the rope

Rope is made by spinning short fibres into a yarn, which is then made into a twisted strand. Most ropes are made of three strands which is known as laid rope. So that the rope can be made flexible and strong,

In and out with the tides

The village of Appledore lies on the south side of the confluence of the rivers Taw and Torridge, and for centuries the residents of the village has turned to the sea for food, fuel and of course a livelihood. Life for these people was governed by the tides, six hours in and six hours out, so depending on the activity which was going to be undertaken, on any particular day it was always the tides and the weather that set the agenda.

Father taught me about tides, where to go fishing at different states of tide, what bait to use and where. I was with no doubt both a son and a daughter to him. I was also a dab hand at wire brushing the bottoms of the boats and painting them (we had four). So I was an Appledore maid by trade! These were all activities in between working full time as a nurse in the operating theatre at the local hospital, and doing on-call duties for three nights one week and four the other. Very often we would be up all night with several emergencies, and then just carry on with the day shift. In those days we had time off in lieu of pay, which meant on days we were not on call we would be given a half a day off. I would ring home and tell my father that I would be home by about one o'clock, he would then go down to the beach and put the boat off, so that it would not go aground with the ebbing tide, and we would then have an afternoon fishing and, if the conditions were favourable, perhaps sieve the water for a 'red hake' (salmon (poached!)) or two.

From time to time a surgeon or an anaesthetist would enquire if there was the possibility of a red hake as their wives were arranging a dinner party or perhaps there was to be a family wedding. We were usually successful in filling the order. I had their private telephone numbers so I was able to inform them that there was going to be a visit.

Single rope strand divided into two further strands (themselves also composed of two strands)

Rope unlaid into three separate strands

Photo 1: laid up rope of three strands which has been unlaid

these three strands are then twisted together in opposing directions. To make a mat it is probably best to start off by using half an inch diameter rope. It makes the handling much easier, and it is advisable to cut it into lengths of about 12 feet.

First unlay or unwind the three main strands of the rope; then take down these individual strands to two strands, thereby making six strands consisting of two strands each. These are the lengths from which the sennit is made (*photos 1 & 2*). A knot should be tied at the ends of these to prevent them unlaying any more.

In order that the working strands are easy to handle when making up the sennit, a bundle is made which is known as a fox. This is achieved by winding the strand around the hand keeping the inner end under the thumb: when the end is reached make a clove hitch around the bundle or fox. When working the bundles into sennit, it is the inner end that is the working end. As the bundle becomes slacker the clove hitch can be tightened. Depending on the size of mat to be made it is advisable to make at least 100 feet of sennit.

A sennit being made from the three bundles of foxes

Photo 2: bundles or foxes ready for sennit making.

When starting off making sennit just lightly tie or whip the three strands together at one end and take the knot out; this prevents it from unlaying any more. Then just plait the strands together, the outside strands over the middle. This is where strong hands are useful as a fair amount of tension is needed. At some stage a new length of strand is going to have to be attached, this is easily done by placing the working end of a new fox over the top of the end of the old fox and plaiting it in as before. It does not matter that a tail is showing as this can be trimmed later. It is best if the sennit can be hitched to something so that a fair amount of tension can be kept whilst plaiting, it is also advisable not to have too much distance between the place where the sennit is hitched and the working end. Once enough sennit is made other items are going to be required to make the mat.

◼ Tools and aids

A reel of good strong twine is essential, it is this that will be holding the mat together and the life of the mat will depend on it. Bee's wax is another aid. The men who made mats at sea in the nineteenth century would have used tallow, which would have been readily available from the galley. When a length of twine is cut from the reel it is pulled over the wax several times coating the twine: the heat from the hands then slightly softens the wax and it acts as a lubricant as the twine is being pulled through the sennit. If the end of the twine is well coated with the wax and flattened between the finger and thumb it makes the task of threading the needle easier.

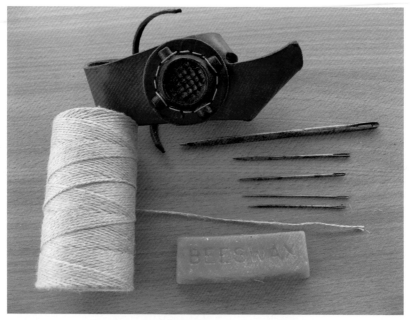

Photo 3: needles, twine, palm and beeswax.

A leather palm and needles are tools used by sailmakers and, of course, saddlers. On board sailing ships the sailmaker was a man whose duty it was to keep the sails and rigging in good running order. In fact he was not required to do any other duties, and on a large sailing ship he would have probably have had a sailmakers mate to assist him. It was the sailmaker whose job it was to sew a dead sailor into his hammock, before sewing him into a canvas shroud along with weights to take him to the bottom. A palm is nothing more than a very heavy duty thimble which fits over the hand and is made of leather (*photo 3*).

Sailmakers needles can be obtained in varying shapes and sizes; most of them have triangular bodies and can be straight or curved. For mat making, needles between the sizes fourteen to eighteen are adequate. Some prefer a curved needle, but it is just a matter of personal preference whether a straight or curved needle is used.

memories of an appledore maid

'living off the beach' – shellfish

Life was hard for those who went to sea, but it was not that much better for those who were ashore; remember, these were times before the welfare state and there often wasn't enough money to put aside for hard times – and retirement was out of the question even if you could find a bit of money to put aside! So the Appledorian expression 'living off the beach' was used. This meant that food as well as fuel would be gathered from the foreshore and the immediate area above high water mark of spring tides. For many families the beach was the main provider of meat in the form of fish or shellfish – limpets, cockles, mussels and winkles were all collected as they came into season. Some of these would be pickled in vinegar to be used at a later date and any surplus would be sold for a few pennies.

CHAPTER 3

Making a rope mat

Starting to make a rope mat can be quite difficult. The end of the sennit has to be made to disappear, and this can be done by whipping the three strands together. If a circular mat is being made then the sennit is made to go around the end and sewn into place, keeping the circular shape; as the mat grows the shape is easier to keep. But it must be remembered that the face of the sennit which is the side showing the lay of the plait should be on the outside. A circle of about 6 to 8 inches is made before any fancy work begins.

■ Stitches

The stitches should be even and be placed into the lay of the sennit so that they cannot be seen, although this is not always possible. Some mats have been made with a light coloured rope, and a darker coloured sewing twine which produces a mat with a pleasing flecked appearance. When coming to the end of the sewing twine the end on the needle should be left so that it is between the sennit which has previously been sewn on, and the sennit which is being sewn on, leaving a long end. Then having threaded the needle with a fresh length of waxed twine, put the needle through the sennit so that the two ends are together, between the two pieces of sennit. Then sew through the sennit, bringing the two tails over and under the stitches two or three times. Doing this makes a tidy and strong joining of the two ends of twine. Once the size of the circle has been reached, the fancy work can begin.

■ Templates and curliques

Templates are used so that the size of the wavy patterns, or curliques as they are called, are not only evenly sized but evenly spaced. On board the old sailing vessels a piece of cork or wood would be carved into an appropriate shape, with a concave inner side that would fit up against the side of the circle. It does not have to fit exactly because the sennit is flexible. The sennit is then sewn to the edge of the circle and tied off, and the template is moved along to the next space. Before starting the curlique work it is wise to ascertain that the template will be able to encircle the mat without too big a gap or an overlap in the pattern. After the first row of curliques are in place, follow these around again with the sennit, this time sewing all around as before. This is usually done about three times as it makes a good firm edge.

Photo 4: template for forming curliques.

After making the curlique it is usual to do more of the plain sennit work, going around about six times. Then more of the curliques are made, but it is important to remember to start making this second set of curliques opposite the place where the first lot were started. Doing this gives an equal pattern to the mat. This process of alternating plain sennit with curliques gives a pleasing, if, simple rope mat.

■ Finishing off around the curliques with plain sennit

To finish off around the curliques, or indeed the mat, eight or ten circles of plain sennit are made around the curliques. A finished mat is usually between 28 and 32 inches, but there is no fixed rule of the size it should be – it depends on the maker and for what purpose or place it is being made for. Finishing off can be done in two ways. The first is by whipping the ends of the sennit with whipping twine and sewing the ends of the whipping twine into the body of the mat, thus securing the end of the sennit onto the mat. Or, secondly, by cutting the sennit longer than is needed when reaching the finishing point, then unlaying the sennit and using a very large sail needle, work the individual strands into the sennit, making sure that the lay is the same. This method can be time consuming and sometimes difficult, but makes an ending to a mat that is virtually impossible to see if done properly.

Photo 5: a simple circular rope mat with alternating plain sennit and curliques

■ Using decorative centre plaits

An Appledore mat usually had an intricate pattern at its centre – probably due to the rivalry between the makers of the mats – known as a plait, and was made separately from the mat itself, the sennit being sewn on after as described above (*photos 6 & 7*). This is a step forward from making the basic circular mat. To make a plait for the centre of a mat it would be advisable to obtain a book on knots and plaits. There are a number of these books on the market, all have good descriptions and easy-to-follow pictures.

It would be advisable to practice making plaits before embarking on using them in a mat, and to use rope about three eighths of an inch in diameter. Favourites used for a centre piece are either an Ocean or Carrick plait. Both make a pleasing intricate design – looking as if there is no ending or beginning.

Photo 6: Carrick plaits to be used for the centre of a mat

Photo 7: a rope mat with a carrick centre

The same rules apply as the description above for making a mat, but first of all the sennit has to be attached to the edges of the plait. This is done by sewing around the outer edges of the plait to the sennit, and leaving gaps where the rope goes into the middle. Leaving a space similar to the ones formed within the plait, it is advisable to do about six rounds before starting on the curliques. This can be a bit more difficult than on the simple circular mat because, the curlique needs to be aligned with the central curves giving the mat a symmetrical pattern.

■ Edge-to-edge sewn mats

The mat technique described above uses sennit sewn side to side but with another method, which is slightly more difficult, the sennit is sewn edge-to-edge. The centre usually has a ocean or carrick plait, but this time sennit is used and not the laid up rope. The sennit must be kept flat when being made up into the plait of choice because it is very easy to twist the sennit, so this is not a method to use unless there has been plenty of practise first. When the plait has been made and is satisfactory for display in the middle of the mat, it is advisable to loosely sew the plait so that the sennit keeps its shape; this also holds the edges down so that heels of shoes are not caught in the turns!

Photo 8: flat or edge-to-edge rope mat

After the plait has been made secure, the ends are finished off either by whipping or by burying the ends using the very large sail needle as described above. Sewing the sennit edge-to-edge is quite difficult; the twine should not be drawn too tight as the edges of the sennit will be drawn over one another causing a ridge. The stitching can be done on the reverse side of the mat, the side that will be on the floor. Curliques can be worked the same way as in the side to side method, but great care is needed to get a satisfactory result, and this can only be learnt by experience.

Using this method to make a mat produces a very pleasing end product, but unfortunately some of the stitches are more visible than in the side-to-side mats where the lay of the sennit can hide them. But this can be used to advantage if a slightly different coloured twine is used, giving a flecked appearance to the work. I have one of these mats which my father made over 50 years ago, and it is still going strong (*Photo 8*)!

memories of an appledore maid

Fishing on the ebb and flood

Fishing: the residents of Appledore have always looked to the sea for food, and fishing with either hook and line or with a net was a means of obtaining food for the family, or indeed to bring in a few shilling. Many households in the village in the early twentieth century did not have a clock, but what they did have was the church clock, which struck the hour, and the tides. Often as a child I would be sent down to the quay to see where the tide was. I would run home and tell Father that so and so's boat was just taking the ground if the tide was ebbing, but if it was flood tide I would report that so and so's boat was fleeting! With this information he would look at our kitchen clock and would calculate the time of the next high or low water, adding the day-to-day variants and weather conditions. So, in the same way, the old residents of the village would know the time by the daily ebb and flow of the tides. The times of high water also told them whether they were neaps or springs.

Most fishermen in the village would fish for about six hours – three hours of the ebb and three hours of the flood tide. If they did not catch anything in those six hours then there was nort about! The nature of the estuary of the two rivers has dictated that the mid-tide times are the best for fishing. But if there were excursions out over the bar to catch Skate or Turbot with long lines, then the crossing of the shallow bar had to be put into the equation, because if the wind was blowing against the tide this would make the crossing hazardous.

CHAPTER 4

Other mats: canvas, knitted, wheel

■ Canvas hearth mats

There are three other types of mats that I can remember my father making. The first one is the mat whereby the strands of the rope are sewn onto canvas. A piece of canvas two feet wide and about six feet long was used. A brass rod – usually an old stair rod – would be used to make the pile. This was done by over-sewing the rod and through the canvas with, usually, two strands of rope. A very large sail needle and a palm was used for this work. When the end of the row was reached the rod was pulled from the over-sewing and the canvas turned over and thumped with a 'thumper'. This was done so that the strands were all even, and worked into the canvas. There are two of these mats in the collection which we gave to Nicola Schnoor.

Photo 9: thumper

Joining in new lengths of the strands was done by working the ends into the stitches on the back of the mat as the other stitches were made, then cutting them short when the mat was finished. This type of mat is hard work, and needs a fair amount of room, we were lucky, as we had a very large kitchen and father use to have one end of the room for his 'met' making.

Photo 10: canvas backed mat

Sailors on the old sailing vessels would have had plenty of room on a deck to be able to make one of these mats and, of course they would have had to hand the materials needed to make it with. The type canvas which my father used is unobtainable today.

At home we had a iron stove known as a bodley, and these were made in the village. There was always a canvas mat on the floor in front of the fire. The bodley stove could be used either as a open fire with the bonnet fitted, or closed down, so that the oven would be heated up and

'living off the beach' – Samphire

Plants, too, were gathered from the beach and sand dune areas of Northam Burrows (now a SSSI), the most popular were the Glasswort or Marsh Samphire (*Salicornia europaea spp*) which was gathered from the mud flats of the Skern, and Rock Samphire (*Crithmum maritimum*) which grew amongst the pebble pavements of Greysands and the pebble strewn sand dunes in other parts of the estuary.

Known locally as 'tabby grass', Glasswort was gathered from the muddy salt marshes of the estuary, usually in the late spring or early summer whilst it was still young and succulent. After it had been washed and gently boiled it was served as a vegetable or it was pickled and used to accompany cold meat. At the end of the summer when the grazing on Northam Burrows was often poor, the sheep would go down onto the Skern salt marsh and graze on the tabby grass, not only finding it good grazing but also receiving some of the essential minerals and vitamins which kept them healthy. As the name glasswort suggests it was used for making glass – a process which involved mixing the ashes of the plant with sand – which was probably introduced to this country by foreign glass makers in the 16th century. There is no evidence of glass making in Appledore.

Rock samphire did not grow as prolifically as the tabby grass, but in the large dune systems of Greysands and on the coastal cliffs some of these plants flourished. These were collected and were eaten raw as a salad vegetable or pickled and used as a relish with meat. Samphire and the earlier 'Sampere' or 'Sampier' is from the French, *Herbe de St. Pierre*, the herb of the fisherman saint whose name was Petros, or rock (St. Peter). This herb, which grows out of the seaside rock or stony ground, and eaten in salad or as a pickle, was considered good for the prevention of stones or troubles with the kidneys or bladder.

Drawing of Marsh Samphire by kind permission of Monti Beale could be used for cooking. The oven door had a brass knob handle for lifting the catch which held it shut: mother would feel this knob to judge the temperature of the oven before putting the knubbies or the schooner on the rocks in to cook. Often when the bonnet was up and the fire was open, a spark from a knot in the wood would spit out and the mat would start to singe! It was probably quite some minutes before we would smell the mat singeing and then someone would get up and stamp it out! It never seemed to damage the mat all that much.

■ The knitted mat

This mat is made on the exact same principles as knitting a jumper or cardigan, but obviously the method and tools which are used are the ones seamen would have had to hand when at sea. No sewing is done until the mat had been made, then it would be embellished with curliques around the edges.

Photo 11: a knitted rope mat made by the late Walter Ford

Equipment and materials needed to manufacture this mat are: half inch diameter manila, hemp or sisal which is laid – old rope of this size would be ideal if it were available; an old brass stair rod about three feet long, or the same length of steel tubing with no more than half an inch in diameter; and a tool which father called his knitting fid.

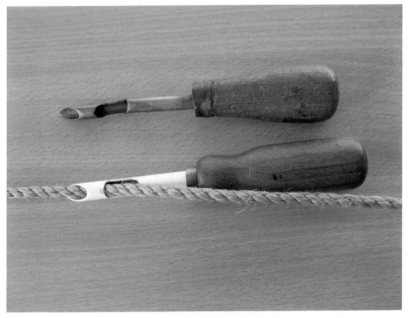

Photo 12: knitting fids

The fid which my father used was made of brass, but unfortunately, is the worse for wear. But my husband has been able to make one almost exactly the same by using a piece of aluminium rod. It is virtually the same diameter as the original, which he was able to marry into an old screwdriver handle.

■ Knitting rope

Making knitted mats is easy if the maker is familiar with the knitting process, but it is very hard work. It is advisable to begin one of these mats with only 12 or 15 stitches cast onto the rod, and practice the process before embarking on making a mat for real. The work can always be ripped out (to use a knitting phrase) and the rope straightened out and used again. As with knitting, measure off enough rope from the coil to use as the casting on stitches. Thread the whipped end of this into the fid and pull through. Place the rod under the left thigh, (if left handed under right thigh), and sit on rod. Sitting on the rod gives the maker both hands free to carry out the work, and the weight of the body will hold the rod firm and steady so that tension on the work can be maintained and kept at a uniform level. The tension should not be too tight or the work will be difficult to get off the rod, nor too slack, as stitches will be dropped.

■ Casting on and knitting

Make a slip knot onto the rod, then using the length of rope for the casting on, make a twist around the left thumb and push the fid through the twist and pull the rope from the end of the fid through and onto the rod. Carry on with this until the number of stitches required has been put onto the rod. Pull the stitches off the rod (it is now that the discovery will be made as to whether the stitches are of the correct tension) and carefully turn the end which has just been finished towards you and push the fid into the first loop. At this point it is important that the work does not become twisted; also it is easy to drop a stitch at this time! Then push the fid through the loop and pull the rope through the fid and through the loop before placing it back on the rod. Keeping both the rope from the fid, and that which is already on the rod, tight. Carry on in this fashion until the end of the row. Then, as before, remove work from the rod, reverse the mat, and knit back onto the rod again as before (*photo 13*).

■ Casting off

Casting off the work from the rod, is virtually the same as casting off when knitting with wool. But all the stitches are taken off the rod as before. The fid is pushed through the first stitch and onto the rod. This first stitch is then lifted over the second stitch: carry on doing this until the last stitch. Then cut the rope leaving about 8–10 inches and thread it through the last loop. Unlay the remaining end, and thread the individual strands one at a time into a very large sail needle and work them into the mat one at a time, in slightly different places. Cut the ends as close as possible to the mat, hopefully showing no ends.

This type of mat can be made into a knitted square, or rectangle. When the knitting has been completed sennit can be applied around the outside. Usually a few rows of sennit is stitched on before any curliques are made. When this has been completed three or four rows of straight sennit is put around the outside to finish the mat.

Photo 13: author knitting a rope mat

■ The 'bicycle wheel' mat

Contained in the V.C. Boyle archive collection of Appledore mats, is a description and a drawing of how a particular type of mat was started off on a bicycle wheel, as told to Mr. Boyle by Captain Tom Scilly. The following is an extract from those notes:

> *"The central part is a tight, close disc exactly 25 inches in diameter. It has whirling patterns on it in green. The whirls are not due to passing the twine spirally. This disc is made in an old bicycle rim. When it is done a border of loop patterns is added. The central disc. 1) Mark the central bike wheel rim with a file so that the two halves are equal. 2) Starting at 1a pass your twine across to 1b. give it a marline hitch, then 3) carry it along one inch to b2 and there have a marline hitch. 4) From b2 go across to 2a then along to 3a, where making a marline hitch, proceed to make another diameter. 5) Carry on like that making marline hitches at every inch and crossing all the diameters atone point in the centre, when nearly finished, look to find if both halves of the circle have an equal number of spokes".*

I am lucky to have in my possession one of these mats. The others which I owned were given to the owner of the sailing vessel *Bessie Ellen*, Nicola Schnoor, née Alford. This came about because, my paternal grandfather was captain of the *Bessie Ellen* and my father sailed with him. When Nicola came back from Denmark in 2002 after carrying out massive restoration work on the old vessel I contacted her, and she invited me down to Plymouth to where the *Bessie Ellen* was berthed. I had several old mats of various types which my father had made, and because I had no room to display them either on the floor or on the walls, on one of our visits I took them down to her. They are now in the safe keeping of the Schnoor/Alford family.

■ How the 'bicycle wheel' mat was actually made

Over the last few months my husband George and I have very closely examined the wheel mat which my father made. We have poked, prodded and counted every round and lateral strand, and eventually have been able to ascertain how this mat was made. My husband has made one of these mats, and without the aid of a bicycle wheel!

Photo 14: bicycle mat made by the late Walter Ford

Appledore men have always had a great sense of humour, or as they called it 'having a bit of fun' with someone. These days it would be called something else! These old boys would probably meet up on Appledore quay for a yarn, and the conversation would inevitably come around to the latest happenings and visitors to the village. They all knew Mr. Boyle because he had been speaking to most all of them about the Appledore mats. So it is a possibility that he was on the receiving end of their bit of fun. We are convinced that the bicycle wheel mat was such having a bit of fun. My father made a number of these mats on our kitchen table, but I do not ever remember him using a bicycle wheel. I can recall some really weird and wonderful things turning up on our kitchen table – but never a bicycle wheel!

In Mr. Boyle's description, at 5 above, he states that all the crossings should be at one point in the middle. We found that in the mats we have examined the spokes were made of two yarns of unlaid rope, which measured approximately one eighth of an inch thick. Now, if sixty-four of these strands crossed at one point in the middle, it would make the finished mat about eight inches thick at the centre. Also Mr. Boyle has said in his written description that twine was used. This material would not have been strong enough, nor indeed could it have been worked in the way this mat is constructed. Twine was material which was used for the sewing together of mats.

After studying Walter Ford's original mat we concluded that it had been constructed like all other mats from the centre outwards. Four lateral strands and the end of the rope which make up the body of the mat are combined to form a cross. The lateral strands pass through the body of the mat, and more are added as the diameter of the mat increases. The final size is decided by the length of the original four strands. All the lateral strands are brought through and hidden by the final rounds, usually by sennit of the mat-makers choice.

During the time my husband, George, was reconstructing the mat, he made notes and took photographs of the different stages. In the next chapter he provides a step by step reconstruction of the making of a 'bicycle wheel' mat.

CHAPTER 5

Constructing a 'bicycle wheel mat'

by George Wells

Unlay a length of about twelve feet of half inch diameter rope into its three main strands. Put two of these to one side as these will become the working strands and form the main body of the mat. Take the third strand and unlay this further down to two strand pieces. Cut four lengths of this two strand rope about a yard long, or longer than the desired diameter of the finished mat. These will become the lateral strands. Lay these four strands down in the pattern of two crosses, with all four strands crossing in the centre (*photo 15*).

Photo 15: beginning a bicycle wheel mat

Make one slightly longer than the rest and put this at the bottom of the crosses. Whip the ends of these laterals using plastic tape (easier than using twine). Take the first of the working strands and place the end in the centre of the cross and, keeping the strands in pattern tie an overhand knot with the longest one to include all the laterals, and the end of the working strand together (*photo 15*). Start by curling the working end from the centre to form a flat disc of rope, as you do this keep the lateral strands in pattern. Thread them through the body of the working strand, easing the working strands apart and being sure to pass two strands under and two strands over the lateral strands. Do this for about six turns or rows.

■ Adding more lateral strands

Next, add two more laterals between each existing strand, do this with some of the two strand rope. Lay the new strands into the working end so that they come through as the others do in the rows which have already been made, two over and two under. Now there will be

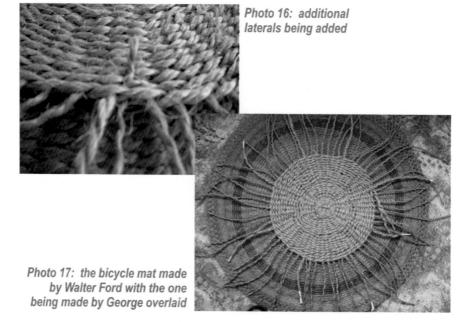

Photo 16: additional laterals being added

Photo 17: the bicycle mat made by Walter Ford with the one being made by George overlaid

twenty-four lateral strands. Continue weaving these through the working strands for another eight rows. Now add more laterals in the same way, put two in between the first two, then two more between the next. Leaving one, and adding two between the next two and so on until you have fifty-six lateral strands.

Photo 16: completed reconstruction of Walter Ford's original wheel mat

■ Keep the lateral strands straight

Try to keep the laterals straight and equally spaced in the working strand. Do six more rows and then add the final eight laterals, laying one in every eighth existing strand gives you the sixty four laterals. Carry on weaving until the desired diameter is reached. The outer edge of the mat can be decorated with some flat edge to edge sennit. To finish, bring your lateral strands through the first round of sennit. Cut these off and sew the second row of sennit to cover and anchor them. A five strand or French sennit makes a good finishing edge.

Photo 18: five strand or French sennit

Making this mat is more of a mathematical exercise rather than just making a normal sennit mat, as it requires the maker to work the strands so that the laterals are straight, and looking as if they had all come from the centre of the mat. But once the technique is mastered and the mat completed it is a beautiful and beguiling piece of work.

'living off the beach' – Laver

Perhaps the most important food commodity that was only available during the winter months, except fish, was Laver (*Porphyra umbilicalis*). Although, technically not a plant, but an algae, it was picked from the pebbles and rocks in the intertidal areas during the winter months by a band of tough, intrepid ladies from the hamlet of Irsha, who between them supplied most all of the families living in Appledore with their winter supply.

Laver – the black gelatinous mass which is often seen today in large bowls in butcher's shops, and is sold locally during the winter months – is a big turn-off for many people. But for centuries it has been gathered, prepared and eaten by Appledorians. It is collected from the stones and rocks of the inter-tidal zones along the coast from Bude (Cornwall) to Westward Ho! beach. It is found more commonly along the western coasts of Britain and Ireland, thus this food source appears to have been a favourite amongst the Celtic races; the same seaweed is called 'Slaak' in Scotland and 'Sloke' in Ireland.

The laver beds are still there in the estuary and people still go out collecting, but over the years the habitats which have sustained the tabby grass and the rock samphire have largely disappeared from Northam Burrows. The sand dune systems and pebble pavements of Greysands and the western end of the Burrows have also gone. And the mud-loving tabby grass of Skern has virtually disappeared because of the accretion of sand which has stifled the habitat. Even if it was allowed to gather these plants from the wild today there would not be enough to sustain even one family – the days of living off the beach have gone.

CHAPTER 6

Rope slippers

In the late 1950's and early 1960's my father made rope slippers. These were made out of sennit and sewn together just like the rope mats. The soles were constructed using the sennit sewn side-to-side, and shaped like bottom of a slipper. A piece of wood shaped into sole and heel of the foot was used as a template. The sennit was then sewn around this until it was easy to handle, the piece of wood was then taken out and the gap was sewn in together, this then gave the basic shape of the foot. The sennit was then worked up from the sole to form the upper part of the slipper, and was then sewn edge-to-edge. A tongue was shaped to come up over the top of the foot, this was made by still using the same length of sennit. The whole of the slipper was made in the same way as the

Photo 20: dolly slippers made by Walter Ford

rope mats, with one long continuous length of sennit. It is unfortunate that we no longer have a pair of this unusual footwear, because when they wore out they were put on the fire! Perhaps I shall try and make a pair in the not too distant future. But we do have a pair of what father called "dolly slippers" (*photo 20*).

Before they were worn in, the roughness of the rope would cause blisters to appear on the heels and toes but, once they were worn in they were very comfortable indeed. I can remember wearing them out of doors and going down onto the quay with them on, but they were not water proof so we did not wear them out of doors when it was wet. And they certainly did not get worn down onto the beach! They were taken off and left on the slipway until we came back from whatever we had been doing.

memories of an appledore maid

Do 'ee want a bit of red hake, me 'ansome?

Poaching for salmon and sea trout was a way of life in Appledore, indeed, in days gone by it was not only a source of income, but also food for the family: 'Not salmon again!' went up the cry. If there had been a successful night's 'fishing', the womenfolk would gut and cut up the fish, and then wrap it up in clean white cloths and carry it to the customers in a wicker basket, knocking on the doors and asking 'Do 'ee want a bit of red hake, me 'ansome?' Salmon and sea trout was called red hake in the village because, it is said, one of these ladies got caught selling the proceeds of the previous nights poaching expedition. She was hauled up before the magistrate, and when she was asked why she was selling salmon out of season, her reply was reported to have been that it was not salmon, 'They' had told her that it was red hake, which was always caught at this time of year. The magistrate, who did not live in Appledore, but was one of her customers, dismissed the case!

CHAPTER 7

End piece: fading traditions

Alas, the days of selling red hake out of season has gone. Gone also are the maids and the boys being taught the skills which were a tradition in Appledore village. A few can still rope and repair a net, but the generations which come after us do not seem to have an interest or the need. They do not have to live off the beach or earn a shilling from the river. My father would have said that they had got too soft! There are one or two villagers who can knit a frock, but even these are no longer youngsters. Unfortunately, they do not use the traditional method of five needles and a tack: today they are knitted on a circular needle. Also in these days of manmade fibres and lightweight clothing it is becoming more and more difficult to obtain the traditional worsted wool.

Like those other traditional skills, rope mat making is also fast becoming a lost craft. There are still a very small number of Appledorians who live in the village and have the knowledge but do not use their skills, and there are those who do not have the time. Making Appledore rope mats is a very time consuming handicraft. But as a skill which was born out of boredom it became both a past-time and a handicraft to all those Appledore mariners who sailed the seas. The rope mats also became a symbol of pride to those who received them; made by their loved ones, they were displayed in the front porch for all to see.

You'm marrying a *Bideford* maid!

Up until the 1939 – 1945 war marriages mostly took place between the families within the village. Occasionally there would be a marriage between a Appledore boy or maid with someone from either Bideford or Northam. In one particular case the boy in question belonged to a real old Appledorian family, and was in his early thirties. The maid was from Bideford. The announcement of the engagement was, as expected, put into the local weekly newspaper, the Bideford Gazette, which was published on Fridays. On Saturday mornings there was a market. This partially covered-in building was constructed with the local materials of cob which contained pebbles in the walls, and the roof was covered by slate, the floor was cobblestones. It was next door to the Appledore newsagents, in the area known as the 'market hill' in Market Street. The Appledore ladies would meet up and have a yarn and catch up with the latest gossip. The mother of the boy who had become engaged was seen by her friend and of course wanted to know who she was. She was told with disgust, that 'Her's a Bideford maid, and that her ain't much to look at, but her's got a burdival [beautiful] set of teeth'. And before her friend could say another word, she walked off. It seems the thought of her son marrying a Bideford maid was all too much!

Inconvenient conveniencies!

In recent years many new people have come into the village to live. They are keen to learn the ways and history of Appledore, but, because they have not been part of that history they cannot appreciate what hardships there were by not having had the experience of living in a coastal village.

As late as the mid-1970's there were still houses in Appledore without modern conveniences. There were not any bathrooms in most of the cottages, an indoor toilet was an absolute luxury, and most cottages only had one cold water tap. I can recall going to work at the hospital one morning when it was particularly cold and announcing that there was ice on the inside of my bedroom window and being looked at with disbelief.

Locals, incomers and a dying tongue

My father's family roots have been traced back to 1634 as being part of Appledore village. And my mother's family tree, which has not yet been completed, will probably show the same time scale of being long term residents of Appledore. My husband, however, was born within the sound of Bow Bells, and he still retains much of the rhyming slang from the East End of London. Half the time I don't know what he's saying, and most of the time he doesn't know what I'm saying! But he has often compared the lifestyle of his father and grandfather, who were lighter or barge men on the London river, to the lifestyles of the fishing and mariner families in Appledore. And he has concluded that the circumstances of living in those times dictated that a shilling had to be made, or a meal had to be provided for the family, by fair means or foul!

Since the second world war the language or dialect of the indigenous Appledorian has changed. Incomers, education and television have eroded dialects all over Britain. There are still a small number of us who speak the Appledore 'tongue', but the children of the village are being taught to speak 'proper'. Local people could tell by the accents where others came from. Bideford, just three miles away is a completely different accent to that of Appledore, and indeed, that of Northamites who are just one mile up the road.

****

SOURCES FOR MATERIALS

For needles and palms:

Bosun's Locker Chandlery
Upton Slip
Falmouth
Cornwall
TR 11 3DQ

Tel. 01326 312212.

www.bosunslockerchandlery.co.uk

For natural fibre rope, sewing twine and palms for both right and left hander's:

Bristol Rope & Twine Co.
80 Feeder Road
St. Philips Marsh
Bristol
BS 2 0TQ

Tel. 0117 977 7033
Fax. 0117 971 7621
E-mail: bristolrope@ukonline.co.uk

www.bristolrope.com

Bees wax can be obtained in one ounce blocks from:

QUINCE HONEY FARM
NORTH ROAD
SOUTH MOLTON
DEVON EX 36 3AZ
Tel: 01769 572401

www.quincehoney.co.uk

ACKNOWLEDGEMENTS

My thanks go to the following individuals: Pat Wiggett, Archivist, North Devon Maritime Museum, Appledore; Charmian Astbury, for her help and advice in writing this book. Monti Beale for kindly allowing us to use the drawing of Marsh Samphire; Mike Towns for his work in putting the book together.

Ann Wells, née Ford, was born and brought up in the village of Appledore, Devon. Her family can be traced back in the village to A.D. 1634. At the age of three months she was taken on fishing trips by her parents out into the estuary of the Taw and Torridge rivers and, at times, across the bar. The fourteen foot clinker-built boat was powered by paddles, which were manned by either her mother or father. But, when the conditions allowed, a lugsail was set. When the lugsail was not being used as such, it became the cradle or hammock for 'the cheel'! So it was from a very early age that she was introduced to all things concerning the river, estuary and boats, including the seasonal changes to the wildlife of the area.

George Wells was born in Essex. He worked for Volvo Penta, and for recreation sailed the Thames estuary. Then with a friend he purchased a powerful motor boat, from which they photographed yachts under sail in the estuary, selling the pictures to the delighted owners.

Photography by George Wells